Brimming with creative inspiration, how-to projects, and useful information to enrich your everyday life, Quarto Knows is a favourite destination for those pursuing their interests and passions. Visit our site and dig deeper with our books into your area of interest: Quarto Creates, Quarto Cooks, Quarto Homes, Quarto Lives, Quarto Drives, Quarto Explores, Quarto Gifts, or Quarto Kids.

First Published in 2021 by Wide Eyed Editions,
an imprint of The Quarto Group.
100 Cummings Center, Suite 265D, Beverly, MA 01915 USA.
T +1 978-282-9590 F +1 978-283-2742 www.QuartoKnows.com

ISBN 978-0-7112-5200-4

The illustrations were created digitally
Set in Arial Rounded MT Bold

Published by Georgia Amson-Bradshaw
Designed by Sasha Moxon
Edited by Georgia Amson-Bradshaw
Production by Dawn Cameron

Manufactured in Guangdong, China CC052021

9 8 7 6 5 4 3 2

It's OK to Make Mistakes

WIDE EYED EDITIONS

"I'm not brave enough. I feel scared," says Little Brown Bear.

"That's OK," says Otter, "being brave doesn't mean not being afraid."

"Being brave means feeling scared, and jumping in anyway."

It's good to try new things.
Maybe they won't work out.
But just maybe...

...they will be the most delicious things you have ever tasted. "Yummy cookies, Rabbit!"

We all have times when think we aren't
clever enough, or good enough.

But there's only one way to really fail:
to stop trying.

"I know I can do it!"
says Little Brown Bear.

Little Brown Bear's coloring doesn't stay inside the lines.

That's OK. It's more important to
have a go than to be perfect.

Little Brown Bear won't win the race.

He doesn't mind.

He knows that, even if he's slow, he's faster than everyone who isn't running!

Little Brown Bear isn't afraid to make mistakes. Why's that?

Because making mistakes is the first step towards getting really good at something.

A big job might feel like it's just too much.
But piece by piece, even the biggest
messes can be tidied up.

Little Brown Bear is as brave a superhero.

When he falls down, he gets up.

When he makes a mistake, he tries again.

"I am proud of myself!" he says.

Great job, Little
Brown Bear!